LEGO Friends

*Seaside Stories

D1142490

Story and art by Blue Ocean Entertainment AG
Friendship Fun written by Olivia London

L B

Little, Brown Books for Young Readers
www.lbkids.co.uk

LITTLE, BROWN BOOKS FOR YOUNG READERS

First published in the United States in 2016 by Little, Brown and Company
First published in Great Britain in 2016 Hodder and Stoughton

1 3 5 7 9 10 8 6 4 2

Stories written by Marisa Reinelt
Pencils and inks by Ignasi Calvet, Fernando Dominguez and Carlos Arroyo
Colours by Miriam Hidalgo and Oriol San Julian

A CIP catalogue record for this book
is available from the British Library.

ISBN 978-1-51020-064-7

Printed in the United States

Little, Brown Books for Young Readers
An imprint of
Hachette Children's Group
Part of Hodder and Stoughton
Carmelite House
50 Victoria Embankment
London EC4Y 0DZ

An Hachette UK Company
www.hachette.co.uk

www.hachettechildrens.co.uk

Welcome to Heartlake City

Heartlake City is the home of LEGO®
Friends, five very different and very
talented girls who are best friends. The
city is centered around a heart-shaped
lake (hence the name!), located directly
between a beach and a mountain range.
This location makes it perfect for all
kinds of outdoor activities like flying,
horse riding, dolphin observing, and
more! The city itself is home to a mall,
a café, a bakery, a vet, a beauty shop,
a swimming pool, and adventure!

Great Places to Visit!

CLOVER MEADOWS
A place where people gather for picnics

CLEARSPRING MOUNTAINS
A mountain range with a spring

MAIN STREET
A great place to hang out with your friends

WHISPERING WOODS
A small forest in Heartlake City

HEARTLAKE STABLES
The horse stables that make up Summer Riding Camp

THE PARK
The Heartlake Dog Show is held here.

HEARTLAKE VET
Injured animals are cared for by the vet, Dr. Sophie.

LAKE HEART
The heart-shaped lake in the center of the city, where people go to swim, fish, and ice-skate

4

HEARTLAKE HIGH
The local school attended by Andrea, Emma, Mia, Stephanie, and Olivia, and all of their friends

PET SALON
A fun place for pets to get pampered

HEARTLAKE SHOPPING MALL
The place for fashion, food, and friends.

LIGHTHOUSE ISLAND
An island off the coast of Heartlake City

CITY POOL
A great place to cool off on a hot day

THE BEACH
The coastline. Emma and Olivia live near here.

5

Andrea

The performer of the group, Andrea is a talented singer and is great at making up her own songs. She loves anything that relates to music: singing, playing the piano, dancing, and the theater. She is a great cook and works at a café. She also has a not-so-secret love of bunnies.

Emma

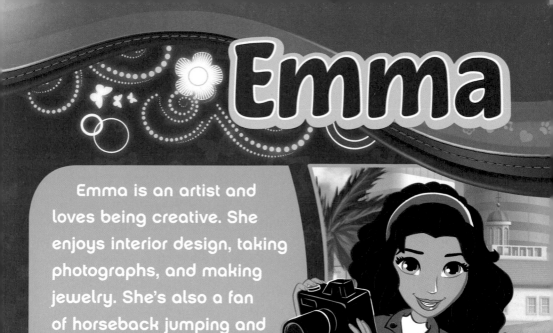

Emma is an artist and loves being creative. She enjoys interior design, taking photographs, and making jewelry. She's also a fan of horseback jumping and karate. She is sometimes forgetful, but she's a wonderful friend.

Mia

The animal lover of the group, Mia enjoys spending time with lots and lots of animals. If she's not training animals, then she's probably taking care of them. She also excels at sports, skateboarding, and playing the drums. In her free time, she rides horses, goes camping, and practices magic tricks.

Olivia

Olivia loves science, nature, and history. If she could, she would spend all day inventing new things, as well as taking pictures and drawing. Super-intelligent and focused, Olivia is quite a brain. She's still clumsy sometimes, but who isn't?

Stephanie

A confident natural leader, Stephanie is very social, creative, and organized. She loves planning events, parties, and soccer. She enjoys talking to people, writing stories, and dancing ballet. Though at times a little bossy, she is very down-to-earth.

AT EXACTLY 3:19...

Oh no! Stop!

Hey, please wait for us!

We want to come too! *STOP!*

Brumm

That was the last bus!

Don't worry, Emma. Maybe someone else is going there and we can catch a ride.

Stephanie, are you clairvoyant?

Honk Honk!

Anyone looking for a lift to the beach?! Here it is!

BUT IT LOOKS LIKE THE FRIENDS CHEERED TOO SOON!

Oh boy, we'll miss the opening if we keep crawling along at this snail's pace! Look at this traffic jam!

Does anyone know a quicker route?

Sure! Just take this forest trail on the left—it's a shortcut!

Are you sure? Because it actually goes in the other direction....

I'm sure! I discovered it last week when I went riding with Bella.

Puff! Bang! Ka-Boom!

Oh no! What's happening to the car?!

I think the engine's had it!

Well, there's nothing we can do without tools.

Let's not waste any more time. We'll leave the car here and just walk the rest of the way.

Best friends forever, forever and ever...

I love that song!

Me too!

Woof!
Woof!

Are you sure about this route? I still think that we're wrong...

Trust me, Steph. I've ridden along here dozens of times with Bella. I know it's right!

A FEW MINUTES LATER...

Gulp! Or maybe not! This river wasn't here last week. I swear!

I told you, Mia. How could you forget about an entire river?!

It's not just her fault, Stephanie! Without your car breaking down, we wouldn't be out here!

We're going to miss the party. Everything is ruined.

Listen up, gang. The sun hasn't set yet.

And arguing isn't going to help. Let's find a solution together or we'll be spending the night here.

I have an idea! Remember gym class last week, when we walked on stilts?

Great idea! We all got the hang of it pretty well. Maybe we can make some...

All we need is some wood that will carry our weight, and something to tie them together...

Yes! It worked! But how are we going to get all our stuff across the river? Walking on stilts is tricky enough without added weight!

And we have to carry Scarlett as well.

I have an idea—we've got towels, right? Let's use them!

Put all the things you want to transport in the middle of the towel and knot two corners together diagonally. Olivia, give me your hair band, will you?

Then, tie the hair band to the corners of the towel, stick your arms through...and you're done!

Woof!

You're a do-it-yourself genius!

Be careful on the rocks—they're slippery!

And be careful over here. It's a bit deeper than before.

Talk about teamwork!

Adventures in Writing!

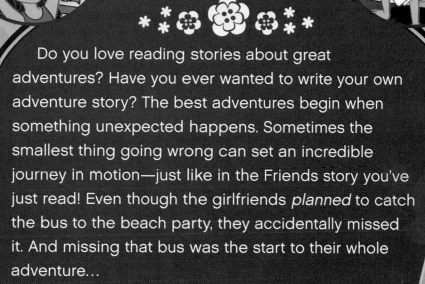

Do you love reading stories about great adventures? Have you ever wanted to write your own adventure story? The best adventures begin when something unexpected happens. Sometimes the smallest thing going wrong can set an incredible journey in motion—just like in the Friends story you've just read! Even though the girlfriends *planned* to catch the bus to the beach party, they accidentally missed it. And missing that bus was the start to their whole adventure...

Craft your own awesome adventure story using these writing tips to guide you!

Location, Location, Location

Choose an exciting location where the adventure will take place. It could be a desert island, a secret city, or a castle in a distant land! Any place that leaves the door open for lots of fun and complicated things to happen is a great choice.

Hero Time *♥*🦋

Figure out who the heroine (or hero) of your story is. Every adventure has one! This character needs to be smart and compelling to grab the reader's attention. A sense of humor helps too! Make sure you know their strengths and weaknesses. That'll help with the story later!

Make an Outline *♥*

Decide what's going to happen before you write. Just a few notes about the whole arc of the story will help you if you get stuck.

The Perfect Plot ★★★

A plot is the series of events that make up a story. There's no right or wrong when it comes to writing, so write a story that you would want to read! Perhaps your character is at a friend's house when she discovers a secret door in the basement that leads to an underground tunnel. Or your character could have planned the adventure from the beginning— like taking a trip to Hawaii to swim with the sharks! Write whatever you want! You're the author!

Move the Story Along

Make sure to include lots of exciting or scary twists and turns! It's this suspense that keeps readers hooked and wanting to read more. Also, it keeps your story moving quickly so it never gets slow or dull. If you get stuck, think of your favorite books or movies. You can find inspiration anywhere!

Climax

A climax is the most exciting part of the book. It's usually right at the end. Make sure your story builds toward an ultimate conflict (this is another word for "struggle" or "fight"). Every good story has a powerful climax moment that should feel bigger than all the other smaller twists and turns—the point at which it seems like all is lost and the hero or heroine won't succeed in their adventure. (But then, of course, they do!)

Share Your Story

Share it with your family or friends. See what they think. Maybe have them write their own story. Or perhaps everyone will love your story so much, you'll have to write the sequel!

Okay, okay, we'll enter it together.

We'll have so much fun, I promise!

Yippie!!!

Annual Sand Castle Competition

Please fill in the form.

What are we going to call our team?

"Best Friends," of course.

HALF AN HOUR LATER, THE CONTEST BEGINS!

Let the Sand Castle Competition begin!

I suggest we build a cute little dog kennel!

Actually, I was hoping we could recreate Livi's dream house. I saw it in a magazine...

It has a heart-shaped pool, an elegant spiral staircase up to the roof, a huge balcony, and...

You can't build that out of sand, Andrea!

Let's build a life-size dollhouse with working doors, windows, and—

Nice idea, but I want more glamour!

AS THE TEAM TALKS, THEY REALIZE IT'S NOT EASY TO AGREE ON AN IDEA DURING A CONTEST.

Hey, did we already talk about my idea? It's really, really good, I promise!

Girls, all the other teams are already hard at work. Let's just build a little house!

A fairy-tale castle with a thousand turrets and—

I don't want to be a spoilsport, but you can't build that with sand, either, Emma!

THE FRIENDS CAN'T AGREE WHAT TO MAKE UNTIL...

We only have twenty minutes!

I've got it: We'll simply take something from each idea!

Exactly! We can build a very simple castle.

With a heart-shaped pool!

With a working door and a dog kennel next to it!

Right, let's GOOO!

The pool collapsed! Mia, will you help me?

Yeah, sure!

Emma, your turrets are sloping! Come on, I'll help you!

Thank you!

ONCE THE GIRLS START WORKING TOGETHER, EVERYTHING BECOMES MUCH EASIER.

24

Make Your Summer Wardrobe!

Summertime is one of the best seasons! School is out, friends are available to hang out, and let's not forget the best part of all—you get to dress up in fun clothes! No bulky coats or puffy sweaters. No clunky boots or giant gloves. If you love fashion, you probably *love* summer clothes. They're bursting with bright colors, fun patterns, and light, comfortable designs (just like the Friends). So, if you're looking for something creative to do with your friends this summer, look no further! Design your very own fashion pieces, whether you need T-shirts, shorts, hats, or...well, anything that would be perfect for a day at the beach or a night by the bonfire. Follow these easy steps.

What You'll Need*:

- ✿ T-shirts, tank tops, shorts, whatever you want!
- ✿ ruler
- ✿ safety pin
- ✿ graph paper
- ✿ pieces of cardboard
- ✿ fabric or embellishing glue
- ✿ tweezers
- ✿ rhinestone jewels
- ✿ fine line marker

*If you don't have already own these items, they can be found at your local arts and crafts store.

What to Do:

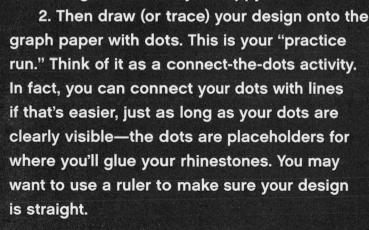

1. Pick a design first! Whether it's flowers or animals or just a cool design, choose something that makes you happy!

2. Then draw (or trace) your design onto the graph paper with dots. This is your "practice run." Think of it as a connect-the-dots activity. In fact, you can connect your dots with lines if that's easier, just as long as your dots are clearly visible—the dots are placeholders for where you'll glue your rhinestones. You may want to use a ruler to make sure your design is straight.

3. Once you've created your design, use the safety pin to poke holes in the paper where you drew your dots. (Be careful with that pointy end!) Make sure the holes are big enough for the tip of the marker to fit through them.

4. Now that all the holes are made, place the cardboard inside the T-shirt to flatten the surface, and place the graph paper with your design on top of the shirt where you want your design to go. Make sure it's placed exactly where you want your design to appear. Then use the marker to mark the dots on the T-shirt through the holes you've made in the paper.

5. Remove the graph paper. You are ready to place little dots of your glue on top of the marks you made on the shirt.

6. With the help of your tweezers, gently place the rhinestones on top of the glue dots to complete your design!

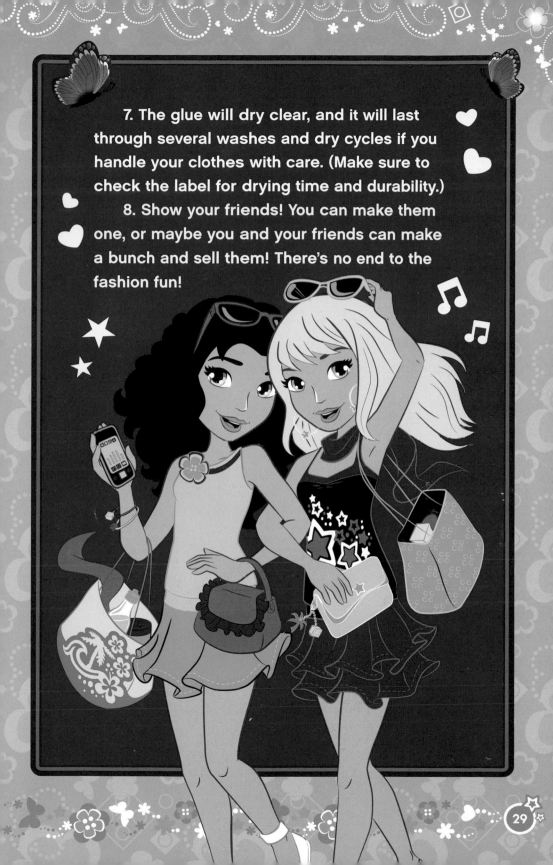

7. The glue will dry clear, and it will last through several washes and dry cycles if you handle your clothes with care. (Make sure to check the label for drying time and durability.)

8. Show your friends! You can make them one, or maybe you and your friends can make a bunch and sell them! There's no end to the fashion fun!

What's Your Perfect Summer?

After training to be lifeguards, friends Andrea and Emma find out that they don't exactly share the idea of the perfect summer job. Emma loves being a lifeguard, while Andrea discovers that it's not the right fit for her. What's your idea of the perfect way to spend your warm-weather months? Take this quiz to find out!

1. **It's a sunny Saturday, and you can't wait to:**

   A. go to the town pool to swim laps. You can't stand not being active on such a gorgeous day!

   B. veg out on the beach or by the pool—with friends of course! It's the weekend! You want to kick back and take in some sun.

   C. spend your Saturday volunteering. Maybe you'll see if the local community center needs your help with anything!

2. True or False: You can't sit still!

A. True, totally. The only way you're spending the day on the couch is if someone chains you to it!

B. Uh…false. (And whoever says true is bananas!) Life is totally hectic, so when you get the chance to sit back and relax, you take it. No questions asked.

C. Depends. You don't *always* need to be running around, but you do want to be productive somehow. Sometimes, reading a good book or helping your neighbors with chores is the best way to relax!

3. **Whatever you end up doing, the most important thing about your summer is:**

    A.   that you spend it challenging yourself. What fun is life without a little competition, and who can challenge you better than new people?

    B.   that you use the time to get closer to your best friends. Summer is a time to solidify those friendships, and make real, lasting memories.

    C.   that you spend it having a real adventure and experience something different from your usual routine. Helping others is always a plus!

4. **The worst thing that could happen to you this summer is:**

    A.   You sleep too much.

    B.   You have to go away and leave all your friends behind.

    C.   It flies by, and you don't have any time to volunteer.

ANSWERS:

Mostly A's:

You're super-active, and you can't stand sitting still. You love trying new things, meeting new people, and exploring new things about yourself and your abilities. Summer is a time to kick your passion into high gear, and there's no time to waste sitting around in front of the TV. Your perfect summer means heading away from home to go to sports or dance camp to hone your skills.

Mostly B's:

You're all about the R and R—rest and relaxation. Vacation is a time to enjoy being carefree, and that's exactly what you're going to do. It's also the perfect time for you to reinforce your friendships and have some quality time with the people closest to you. After all, one day you might move away and you'll wish you'd cherished this time together. Your perfect summer means sticking close to home and basking in the sun arm in arm with your besties!

Mostly C's:

You want to experience the world by helping others. You are particularly interested in participating in something that's focused on the greater good. You love giving back and aiding those who have less than you. Your perfect summer means volunteering, either locally or somewhere outside your home! (Just make sure your parents know where you are at all times!)

Treasure Hunt!

THE FRIENDS NOTICED THAT THEIR BIOLOGY TEACHER, MISS MAIER, IS VERY SAD TODAY. THEY ASK HER WHAT'S WRONG.

I lost my engagement ring at the beach. I'm planning a search party tomorrow.

We'll help you!

That would be wonderful. The more help, the better. I'm really worried I'll never see my ring again.

Clap!

Scribble

But how are we supposed to find the ring? The beach is huge!

We'll just grab some really big shovels and dig our way through the whole beach. Hee-hee!

No way! The shovels might disturb the animals that live on the beach!

Calm down, Mia! Let's meet up later at my place and we'll find a solution together.

Take a look at this, Emma!

We found something that should help locate that ring!

What is THAT weird-looking thing?

A metal detector? Aren't the magnets dangerous for the animals?

Mia's right—we should be considerate of the wildlife.

Whatever we do, we have to be careful not to harm any animals!

Don't worry. I'll give Miss Maier a call and ask her.

That's a great idea! Miss Maier would know. She's a biology teacher after all!

Exactly!

Andrea, Emma, you go get some shovels.

The rest of us will get the metal detector.

Are you sure the animals will be okay?

Of course! We'll make sure they take priority. Plus, it'll be nice to help our teacher!

My uncle just e-mailed me back, and he'll let me borrow his metal detector! He showed me how to use it last summer.

That's great. I'll drive us over there so we can get it.

And I'll hop online and see what kind of wildlife we need to look out for. This is going to be an adventure!

LATER...

Okay, we're all here. Let's start!

Wow!

Okay, here is the plan: Everyone searches in his or her own section. Call me when you find something!

Come on, Andrea, show me your best camera smile!

Shriek!

Shriek!

Dig

Mia, look!

Miss Maier, I think we found your ring!

I hope so...I've been searching all morning, and all I've found is an old wire basket.

Well, it's definitely pretty enough to be an engagement ring.

Oh, wow! Girls, this really is my ring! You're the BEST!

Oh boy, she is *sooo* happy!

No surprise! But who's the owner of the watch?

Giggle

Let's continue our search and give everything we find to the lost-and-found office.

Then, we can create an online post telling people to check for lost items!

Just imagine what else we could find! Wallets, wedding rings, valuable heirlooms...

We'd better get started if you want to find all of that, Miss Treasure Hunt!

Listen to all that beeping! Maybe you discovered a treasure chest!

Hey, hey, step back, Columbus! I haven't even started digging yet.

Beep! Beep!

Oh, look, an old medallion! It's really pretty.

It's okay. Real treasure would have been better.

This is more beautiful than every gold treasure! So cute!

A FEW HOURS LATER...

LOST PROPERTY

Okay, everything's at the office now.

See you at Stephanie's tomorrow!

Green Sea Turtles

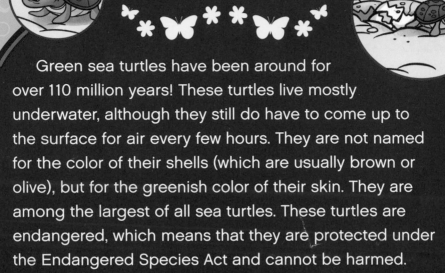

Green sea turtles have been around for over 110 million years! These turtles live mostly underwater, although they still do have to come up to the surface for air every few hours. They are not named for the color of their shells (which are usually brown or olive), but for the greenish color of their skin. They are among the largest of all sea turtles. These turtles are endangered, which means that they are protected under the Endangered Species Act and cannot be harmed.

What do they eat? Young green sea turtles eat worms and small crustaceans as well as plants and algae. Once the turtle reaches adult age, it becomes an herbivore and will only eat plants and algae.

Where do they live? Sea turtles live primarily in warm or temperate waters, with a large population residing around Australia and Costa Rica.

© BlueOrange Studio/Shutterstock.com

How do they communicate? Sea turtles speak to one another with grunts, chirps, and other mixed sounds. Scientists have even found that baby turtles make noises to communicate to one another while still inside their eggs!

Are they good swimmers? Sea turtles can hold their breaths for an incredibly long time—up to five hours sometimes!—making them ideal for deep underwater swimming. Their flippers are strong and wide to help them steer, and they are known for swimming great distances during migration, as far as 1,400 miles.

How long do they live? The lifespan of a sea turtle is extremely long—up to eighty years!

How big are they? Green sea turtles can get as big as five feet in length, and can weigh as much as seven hundred pounds.

Did you know? Female green sea turtles will choose the same spot where they were born to lay and nest their own eggs. They will lay approximately 115 eggs at a time. Wow!

Unexpected Help!

NORMALLY, THE FRIENDS LIKE TO DO THINGS TOGETHER. BUT TODAY THEY'RE EACH SPENDING SOME TIME ALONE BEFORE THEY MEET UP AT A BEACH PARTY IN THE EVENING.

It is such a beautiful day!

WOOSH

It's nice to be biking on my own today. The others would never have dared some of these stunts!

Now for a jump. Aaaaaaaaaaand...

...GOOOOOOO!

Hmm. Maybe I should ask them if I can play...?

Oh no, better not! I don't know them and they're older than me too.

BANG

Oops. I missed!

Eva, you need to step up your game!

mmpf

Thanks!

You're welcome...

Bye, Olivia! Keep in touch!

See you soon!

I can't believe I was scared to talk to them at first. They were so nice.

I'm glad I asked if I could play. It's always nice to make new friends.

Oh, a text message.

Bzzzzz

Hey, honey! Sorry, had a flat tire! Don't be angry! :(

Of course I'm not mad!

No prob! C U tonight! :D

Hmm. That gives me an idea...

Giggle!

End

Don't Give Up!

Shriek!

Shriek!

Shriek!

Swoosh

MIA WENT OUT FOR A LONG RIDE ON BELLA THIS MORNING AND NOW SHE'S SPENDING THE REST OF THE AFTERNOON SURFING.

Woo-hoo! Great waves today and almost no one here. Fantastic!

Hi, Mia!

Hey, Kate! Great waves today, right?

Oh yeah, here it comes!

Whoa, it's too big!

A dolphin! This day isn't full of bad luck—it's quite the opposite!

Hello! What have we got here?

A message in a bottle! I wonder who sent it!

I'll open it on the beach. I can't wait to find out what it says!

Splish Splash

End

What Must Be, Must Be!

EMMA LOVES BEING A LIFEGUARD. BUT TODAY SHE ISN'T ENJOYING HER JOB AS MUCH AS USUAL...

Bah! Stupid beach cleanup duty!

Giggle

It's certainly not the most fun, but cleaning up is part of the job!

I know. All the trash left behind by visitors can't just be left lying here.

But it's still yucky.

EEWWW!

Look at that!

Exactly. Otherwise no one would want to come to the beach.

I don't believe it: a hot dog! Who would toss it on the ground when there's a trash can a few feet away?

I don't know. It's just disgusting!

We're lucky I've got my special tool!

I'm prepared for everything! If you knew some of the things I've found here!

I don't even want to know! Thank you!

There. Clean as a whistle again!

The beach looks spotless! Are you going to the party tonight?

Yes, I've been looking forward to it all day! I'm going with my friends. That reminds me, I'd better text them.

My sister's coming too. It'll be a blast!

Can't wait 2 C U all @ the beach party! :)

Send

True Friends!

ANDREA WROTE A SONG FOR HER FRIENDS. AND SHE'S PERFORMING IT AT THE BEACH PARTY TONIGHT.

WITH HER FRIENDS SUPPORTING HER, ANDREA ALWAYS PUTS ON A GREAT PERFORMANCE!

I hope Emma and the others like my surprise song!

AN HOUR LATER, ANDREA IS BACKSTAGE...

Yikes, that's a lot of people!

Say cheese!

Let's get this party started!

When is it gonna start?

What is wrong with me? I don't normally have stage fright like this!

Hey, are you the next singer?

What if the crowd doesn't like my song? What if they boo me off stage?

Maybe I should have sung my song to someone first...

Oh, sorry, I'm just waiting for my friends.

What are you waiting for?

No! I can't do it! I can't get out there!

Dolphins

* ♥ * ✿ 🦋 * ♥ *

These beautiful marine animals are known for being extremely intelligent and very playful. Dolphins are also mammals, just like you! This means they have to swim to the surface periodically to breathe in air. Dolphins are an endangered species, just like green sea turtles. If you want to impress your parents and friends, read on for some amazing facts about dolphins!

What do they eat? Dolphins are carnivores, and feed mostly on fish and crustaceans.

Where do they live? Dolphins live all over the world, mainly in tropical or more moderate water temperatures.

How do they communicate? Dolphins speak to one another much like humans do. They use certain sounds such as clicks, whistles, and squawks in a variety of patterns to communicate different things to one another.

They can make as many as one thousand sounds per second! Some scientists suspect their language is quite advanced. For example, they are able to express a warning about sharks hunting nearby.

Are they good swimmers? Dolphins are extremely good and agile swimmers. They are known for the advanced tricks they can pull off—like flips! The bottlenose dolphin has been observed breaching up to sixteen feet above the water, landing with a splash on its back or side. Some dolphins can swim up to twenty miles an hour!

How long do they live? Dolphins can live up to fifty years, but somewhere between thirty and forty is the most common.

© Willyam Bradberry/Shutterstock.com

How big are they? Dolphins can grow to be around eight to thirteen feet long. And they can weigh over one thousand pounds.

Did you know? Like bats, dolphins use *echolocation* to track their prey. That means their sounds travel until they reach objects (or creatures), then bounce back and report the location, size, and shape of what they've encountered.

The LIGHTHOUSE Trip

AS PLANNED FOR WEEKS, THE GIRLS ARE GOING TO CAMP OVER THE WEEKEND IN THE BAY NEAR THE LIGHTHOUSE.

Do we have everything?

I hope so. My backpack is stuffed full!

Then it's time for the air taxi to take off!

This is going to be a fantastic weekend!

SWOOOSH

AFTER THEY PARK THE PLANE...

Shall we put the tents up now?

How about we go swimming first?

Let's do it!

SPLISH SPLASH

I'm going for a walk.

Huh? Yeah, okay!

Does anyone want to play beach volleyball?

Shriek!

I'm trying not to feel sorry for myself, but it doesn't look like my friends planned anything special. Have they forgotten that today is my **birthday**?!

I'm free!

Pass to me!

THE AFTERNOON PASSES IN NO TIME.

Andrea, come over here. It's time we put the tents up!

Yes, otherwise we will have to sleep in the sand.

Does it go in there or there?

Let's swap. Mine doesn't fit, either.

Do you think those two are ever going to get it?

No, but I think the tent is. Hee-hee!

Insert the poles and connect them to the roof.

I think I figured it out!

We did it!

YES!

CLAP!

We are the best!

And you thought we couldn't manage it. Ha!

That's right. Ha! Hey, what's so funny?

RUMBLE!

Aww, nooo!

It was a great idea to come here.

Any big plans for the evening?

Wink!

What? We'll relax by the fire—that's the plan!

Crackle!
Crackle!

Just look at that sunset!

It's like a postcard!

They really seem to have forgotten about my special day...

Uh-oh, the fire is going out.

Yes, we need to get some wood before it gets dark.

Andrea, it's your turn. Do you mind collecting some wood?

sigh
Of course.

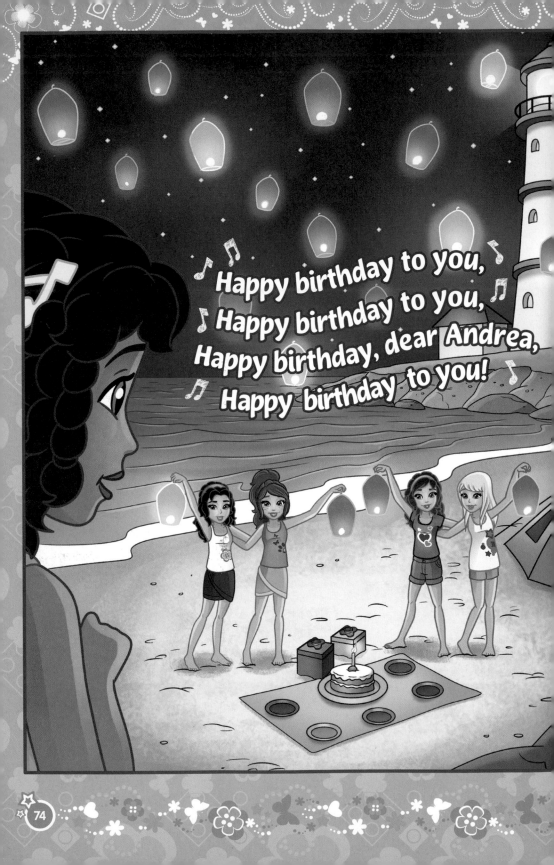

1...2...3... SURPRISE!

Most people love a good surprise party—especially when the guest of honor is a close friend. Surprise parties are a fun and thoughtful way to show someone just how much you care about them. Follow these easy tips for how to throw the best surprise birthday party ever, and you'll be jumping out from behind a couch screaming, "SURPRISE!" in no time.

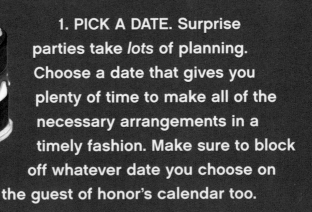

1. PICK A DATE. Surprise parties take *lots* of planning. Choose a date that gives you plenty of time to make all of the necessary arrangements in a timely fashion. Make sure to block off whatever date you choose on the guest of honor's calendar too.

2. PICK A PLACE. Find an easy and safe location for the party. Remember, you're going to have to find a way to get the guest of honor to this location without raising too many questions, so make sure the destination is something you can weave easily into a fake story!

3. BE SPECIFIC. On the invitation, list the time the guests should arrive and the time when you expect the guest of honor to arrive. Be sure to ask your guests to arrive at least thirty minutes *before* the guest of honor. This will give them time to settle in and hide before the surprise. It also ensures that if any guests are running late, they will know to wait until after the surprise is over to enter the party.

4. DON'T SPOIL THE SECRET.
Make sure all of the guests invited to the party *KNOW IT'S A SURPRISE!* After all this planning, the last thing you want is for someone to spill the beans to the guest of honor by accident because they didn't know it was supposed to be a secret.

5. PICK A CHAPERONE. Place one person in charge of getting the guest of honor to the party location under the guise of another activity. You can do it, but if you ask someone else to handle that part, you are free to make sure the rest of the party runs smoothly!

6. PICK UP YOUR PHONE. Don't ignore calls or messages from the guest of honor the day of the party! If you ignore these attempts at contact, the guest of honor will get suspicious. Answer as if it's just an ordinary day, and it will go a long way in preserving your surprise. It also helps in case of an emergency.

7. SNACKS AND DECORATIONS. Don't forget to make the atmosphere festive! Chips and pretzels are a classic, but nuts and veggie sticks are a healthy option. Don't forget some drinks, either. Make sure to get something your guest of honor would like. If they are gluten-free or have a nut allergy, take that into account! If they're gluten-free, cake is out. If they don't like sweets, maybe a fruit assortment is the way to go. Whatever you do, make sure the guest of honor feels at home.

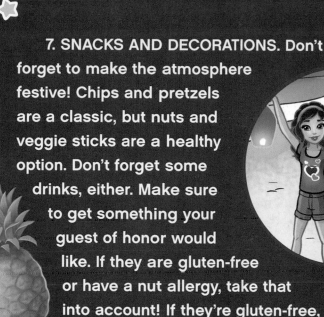

8. TELL EVERYONE WHAT TO YELL BEFORE! This is a rather important point. If it's a surprise birthday, everyone can scream, "HAPPY BIRTHDAY!" If it's an anniversary or something else, make sure everyone is in the know. And remember, have a wonderful time!